CONTENTS

INTRODUCTION

You will often find that many people, in general, will easily come up with their own business ideas. Regardless of how simplistic or complex the ideas are, it is enough to suggest that people can think of good ways to earn a living and become independent. But then why is it the case that only few have the understanding and experience to translate their business ideas into tangible, successful, business realities?

That is because many start their businesses without paying enough attention to the wider details that can have a large impact on their business activities. As a result, they either encounter substantial difficulties or simply get forced out of the market.

Regardless of whether you choose to convert your business ideas into a reality or not, there are a range of issues and thought processes that must be taken into account in order to enlarge your business operations. As the saying goes 'the devil is in the details' and it is these very details that entrepreneurs often do not take into consideration.

ABOUT THIS BOOK

This E-book is aimed to be a thorough guide for entrepreneurs as well as established businesses for growing their business idea or enterprise around the acronym, COPE.

COPE refers to the concepts, objectives, planning and execution of a business. These are detailed as follows:

1) *Concept*: the main idea, feature or characteristic of a business
2) *Objectives*: the targets or goals a business sets to materialise its corporate strategy
3) *Planning*: the business departmental frameworks used to accomplish company objectives
4) *Execution*: ensuring that all business plans are implemented effectively and efficiently

The E-book divides the 4 elements of COPE into 4 chapters detailing the different aspects and areas important for growing or starting your business.

CHAPTER 1: CONCEPT

UNDERSTANDING BUSINESS CONCEPTS

As mentioned earlier, a business idea can be thought of by any person. However, what many people often have trouble with is to change their business idea into a business concept. A business concept forms an outline of how a business will work. It requires delving deeper into questions pertaining to who is the target customer, how a firm's products and services should stand out from rivals and how marketing and supply chain decisions should be adopted by the business.

Clarifying the business concept offers many benefits to both the entrepreneur as well as the company's stakeholders such as customers, suppliers and shareholders. The clearer the business concept is to the entrepreneur, the easier it is for him or her to communicate the value of the business to different stakeholders.

An example of a business concept would consist of providing a little more information than the type of business you are thinking of establishing or expanding. For instance, to say 'I want to begin a restaurant business' does not tell much about the type of restaurant you wish to set up nor the target market your business caters to. However, to say 'I want to establish a restaurant offering quality Chinese cuisine to the high income customer segment' is more fitting.

Start with a business concept statement

To turn your business idea into a business concept, there are a couple of questions that you would need to answer yourself. These include the following:

- What is the product or service?
- What need or gap does the product fulfil?
- How is it superior to other similar products or services?
- Which customer segment will buy the product or service?
- How should the product or service be marketed to the target customer?
- Who are the main rivals in the industry or market?

The aforementioned questions will help to convert your business idea into a business concept. It is important to note however, that the business concept may undergo multiple revisions as you conduct market research and become more acquainted with the different factors and issues shaping your business vision.

Nonetheless, the purpose of the business concept is for you to be able to clearly and accurately describe the nature of the business in two or three lines and form a general picture of the scale of business opportunities and threats.

After you have identified a particular business concept, you can begin exploring the different elements in more depth such as the nature of the market, the customer segment you wish to target and how to position yourself for greater competitive leverage.

KNOW THE MARKET

The most important task you can do before launching or growing your business is to know the market in which you wish to launch and sell your products and services. It is essential that one comes to grip with the market structure, issues, opportunities and threats in the industry.

Market gaps can also be identified that can serve as lucrative opportunities for entrepreneurs and CEOs of well established businesses.

You can employ either field research such as surveys, focus groups or field observations or simply rely on secondary research sources such as market reports, government statistics and so on. Primary field research can be very time-consuming and expensive; however, it can reflect accurate, up-to-date market trends and information.

It is important that entrepreneurs must conduct a thorough market research that will provide them the useful knowledge and insights relevant for their business. Crucial details on the number and type of competitors and customers are very useful for making sure that your business concept statement is accurate and in conformity with the business environment.

A competitor analysis should also be utilized to not only know the strengths of the competitors, but also to know how they execute critical business practices such as marketing campaigns, hiring and training and customer service.

IDENTIFYING THE TARGET MARKET

Utmost attention and time should be given to identifying the right target market, unless you wish to cater to all market segments. Firms who approach carefully sliced, particular market segments can generally occupy greater market dominance and profits.

Owners must therefore pay close attention to how their customers behave, what influences their purchase decisions and what are the best ways to engage and interact with them. This will vary according to the segmentation criterion you adopt.

For instance, the buying habits of the 16-25-year-old age group will vary significantly from the 45-60 one. Factors such as access to internet and culture will play important roles in shaping attitudes among different customer segments.

STRATEGIC POSITIONING

After you have identified the critical areas of the market in which you wish to promote your products and services and the nature of your competitors and customers, it is important to consider strategic positioning for higher competitive advantage.

The all-time famous Harvard business and strategy guru, Michael Porter wrote much about the importance of firms positioning their business operations strategically in a way to maximize their profitability whilst minimizing competitive and other market pressures.

His famous '5 forces model' is a useful, easy to understand guide for businesses to mitigate threats and raise their competitive leverage. The framework serves as an important tool for conducting a structural market and competitive analysis to evaluate the extent to which a firm's profitability can be impacted, either positively or negatively, by the market conditions. This model includes the following 5 considerations:

1) Bargaining power of customers
2) Bargaining power of suppliers
3) Threat of new entrants
4) Threat of substitute products
5) The intensity of competitive rivalry in the market

BARGAINING POWER OF CUSTOMERS

The bargaining power of customers relates to how much control customers can dictate in the market. The higher the bargaining power of customers, the less ability your business has in leveraging profits. This involves analysing how concentrated the group of buyers are and how substantial the goods or services consumed represent as a proportion of their overall costs and other factors.

In essence, to maximise profit potential, the customers' low bargaining power should be characterised by high switching costs. This refers to the ease at which customers can move to another supplier or rival. If switching costs are very low, you will have a harder time capturing customers as they can easily change their suppliers on the basis of low price and higher quality.

Also, if the products or services offered by firms are not differentiated, customers can look for other suppliers more readily. A market characterised by branded goods makes it less easy for customers to switch to another business. Also, this is further impacted by the presence of quality-conscious customers and their lack of knowledge of market prices, costs and demand.

In short, you can choose to increase your profit potential by entering in markets where switching costs are low initially and by branding your products or services, the switching costs increase.

BARGAINING POWER OF SUPPLIERS

The bargaining power of suppliers is an equally important determinant for reducing your profit potential. If suppliers in your industry have control over the prices of raw materials, they can easily threaten to raise prices or reduce the products' quality.

This can have an adverse impact on your ability to earn higher profits.

The bargaining power of supplies can be understood by firstly looking at their concentration in comparison to buyers. If suppliers are less in number than buyers, then they can influence greater control on input prices.

Another reason that could contribute for greater bargaining power of suppliers is access to latest and advanced technologies or expertise that is unmatched by other suppliers in the market. Furthermore, if the raw materials or parts that they provide are differentiated due to branding or other factors and if there is no availability of substitute products, then it can be very difficult for you to negotiate prices to your advantage.

In summary, you can decide to enter markets where suppliers are higher in number relative to buyers, offer standard, undifferentiated components, spare parts and raw materials and where substitutes are readily available.

THREAT OF NEW ENTRANTS

Threat of new entrants relates to how strong the market barriers to entry are in limiting the entry of potential competitors. Markets where barriers to entry are low are often lucrative markets for many entrepreneurs to enter and quickly earn high market share.

High barriers to entry such as economies of scale, presence of strong established brands and high entry and exit costs all can prevent a potential entrant from entering the market. This is because the cost efficiencies and competitive advantages of established firms in the market will be very difficult for new entrants to counter against. In other cases, established firms have better access to distribution channels and have a stronger and more loyal customer base.

For instance, firms who enter the new market can easily be forced out of it following the incumbent firms' decision to lower prices. The fall in prices will not impact the incumbents as adversely owing to low cost scale benefits. However, for the new entrant that has already invested a large amount of capital coupled with little or no sales revenue it will find it extremely challenging to continue conducting business activities.

You would be better off entering a market where:

- Brand names are not powerful enough
- The requirement of initial capital investment is low
- Getting access to distribution channels is not challenging
- Low legal barriers such as patents
- The market has undifferentiated products
- Economies of scale does not determine profitability

THREAT OF SUBSTITUTE PRODUCTS

The availability of substitute products can also have a major impact on raising or lowering your business' profitability. A substitute product is any product that can be purchased as an alternative to the one supplied by a business.

Substitute products also influence switching costs; the closer the substitutability between two products, the lower the switching costs and the easier customers will find another product that fulfils a similar need. The players in the oil market have large been profitable due to the unavailability of close substitutes.

An example of this would be a firm operating as a juice retailer in the summer where a possible substitute could be ice creams. If the retailer raises the prices of its juices, then depending on how close the substitute is to its juices, customers can easily switch to other businesses selling ice creams lowering the sales and profit levels of the juice retailer.

More importantly, the degree of substitutability can be affected by the quality of the product. For instance, in the case of juices, if its quality is far superior to the ice creams offered by rivals, then customers will be less price-sensitive to the price of juices.

Hence if you are looking to enter a market, then you would be better off where no substitute product is available, performance of the substitute is inferior to the product or service offered and where switching costs for consumers are high.

THE INTENSITY OF COMPETITIVE RIVALRY IN THE MARKET

Most important of all, the intensity of competition in the market is also a factor. Any entrepreneur is keen on finding out the number and strength of players already operating in the market. There are multiple ways of assessing the nature of competitive rivalry and the impact it can have for your business.

You firstly need to look at the number of players in the market. The lower the firms, the higher likelihood that competition will be low. This is true in the case of oligopolistic market structures where a few players are dominant and have substantial scale economies and competitive advantages in the form of differentiated products that leads to reduced competitive pressures.

Other factors such as high barrier and entry costs and high consumer switching costs can also discourage potential entrants from entering the market that enlarges the slice of the market share each firm can obtain. Alternatively, slow industry growth and high fixed costs can raise the intensity of the competition.

Therefore, as an entrepreneur, you should be looking to position your business in a market where competition is less intense. This can help you make profits and also break-even a lot quicker and allow yourself to capture a customer base with relative ease.

UNDERSTAND HOW DIFFERENT BUSINESS FUNCTIONS COME INTO PLAY

After completing a market analysis, it is essential to become familiar with the basics of different business functions and activities that will have to be undertaken in your new business. This pertains to the resources, capabilities, costs and strategies required for effective planning and execution.

This is important to understand how revenue streams will be made and how value creation can occur across the entire supply chain. What you need will depend on the results you found using the 5 forces model.

For example, if threat of substitutes and intensity of competitive rivalry is high, then you will have to explore more strategic ways of leveraging assets, skill-sets and clever strategies. How can we ensure that production leads to minimal waste? How should marketing be used to increase customer acquisition and retention rates? And how can the sales team build stronger customer relationships?

These are some of the questions that you as an entrepreneur need to begin asking to be able to make a thorough business plan and model.

BUSINESS MODELS AND BUSINESS PLANS

BUSINESS MODEL

The business model you choose will highlight key features and distinctions. It is important to use clever ways of formulating business models to gain maximum competitive leverage. Many companies such as Amazon.com, Zara and Facebook have thwarted the waves of their competition by designing models in ways that have enabled them to achieve tremendous growth and profits.

One of many examples of this is the online shoe retailer firm, Zappos. Not many would assume that a shoe retailer can become successful by operating online. However, Zappos defied people's expectations. It designed its business model to gauge relationship marketing which put a great emphasis on building strong, long term relationships with its customers. This resulted in its business' rapid growth causing many of its customers to shop from its website repeatedly to the point that three quarters of its customers were repeat buyers.

Therefore, a business model should as a comprehensive descriptive tool that provides details on what is your business, what value you offer to your customers and how single or multiple revenue streams are made. It describes whether your business operates as a 'bricks and mortar', 'clicks and mortar' or both.

More importantly, it should be an extension of the business concept but with a more practical focus in terms of value adding activities and revenue generation flows. Great emphasis should be put on defining and detailing customer value and ensure how a business' value chain can continually provide value to the consumer.

In addition, it needs to stress on particular service features such as customer satisfaction, speed of service or superior quality as its distinguishing feature. Through this, it can allow itself to stand out from its rivals and occupy a significant percentage of the market.

BUSINESS PLAN

Making a business plan can offer you many advantages too. It can help you answer why exactly are you in the industry you have selected and also provide a snapshot of the various marketing, operations and production strategies you have chosen to effectively operate in the market.

The aim of the business plan should essentially be to offer the details of your business. It should include how a marketing department will carry out its objectives, how different departments will coordinate with one another to achieve tasks and what are the ways through which competitive pressures can be mitigated.

It will, moreover, explain the financial health of your business and future expectations. In essence, the business plan will be a supplement of the business model by identifying the ways through which the business model's goals can be achieved.

CHAPTER 2: OBJECTIVE

The aim of any business objective should essentially be to translate your vision and concept of your business into a tangible reality. Having clearly defined objectives and goals helps your company to start its operations on a solid footing and act as a criterion for success. The objectives you set will vary in accordance with the resources and capabilities you possess, the particular corporate strategy you have chosen and in what time frames your objectives fall into.

More importantly, your objectives should fit your business concept, business model and plan like a glove. Any goal set that is contrary to your business model and business plan will derail the success of your business. It is therefore essential that the right business objectives are defined and set.

RESOURCES VS. CAPABILITIES

The first determinant in helping you set your business objectives are your resources and capabilities. The way you decide to leverage your resources and capabilities will have an impact on your choice of strategy. This is because effectively utilizing your business' resources and capabilities leads to pinpointing of strategic competitive advantages that are instrumental in leveraging a greater competitive edge over rivals.

A firm's resources include things that help enable production of the business' goods or services. Resources include working capital and physical assets such as equipment, land and raw materials. Capabilities, on the other hand, are a special type of resources that a firm develops over time. An example of a firm's capabilities includes skills, expertise and experience of its staff and company processes and structures.

After identifying your resources and capabilities, you can turn them into competitive advantages. A competitive advantage gives you an edge over your rivals and can help you gauge higher profits. Developing a competitive advantage involves utilizing resources and capabilities which are valuable, rare, inimitable, durable and complex.

Valuable: How valuable are your resources and capabilities to your target customer?

Rare: How rare are your resources? Do existing players in the market have it? Will potential entrants be able to attain the resource?

Inimitable: Are your resources and capabilities unique? Can it be substituted by rivals in another industry?

Durable: Is your resource or capability temporary? Will it last for very long periods of time or will it be consumed or become obsolete quickly?

The aforementioned factors will help you decide on how sustainable your competitive advantage is. If you can combine resources and capabilities that are valuable, rare, inimitable and durable, then you can have a long term competitive advantage. This will help determine your strategy and the objectives you will set for each of your departments.

PERFORM A SWOT ANALYSIS

To identify your resources and capabilities, it is advised for you to use a planning tool such as a SWOT analysis.

Performing a SWOT analysis will help you focus on how your internal strengths and weaknesses should be aligned with the external opportunities and threats to your advantage.

The aim of the analysis is for you to convert the weaknesses and threats into strengths and opportunities. Alternatively, you can help find a potential competitive advantage by matching your internal strengths with external opportunities.

An example of an internal strength could be the availability of resources such as capital, assets such as land or buildings or expertise in talent acquisition. Opportunities of the SWOT analysis could be demand for large retail store and weaknesses could relate to the lack of experienced staff or employees while the threats could be the higher cost advantages of rivals.

The SWOT analysis should not only be used to identify what internal resources and capabilities you have, but also direct you to acquire strategic resources and develop capabilities that will allow to continually maximize opportunities and minimize threats and weakness.

CHOOSING A BUSINESS STRATEGY

A business strategy is critical for the successful planning and implementation of your business goals and objectives. However, what is most important is what strategic choices or directions you want for your business? Do you wish to base your business around a niche marketing strategy, a cost-focused strategy or a quality-focused strategy?

Whatever strategy direction you choose for your business will dictate how you should organize your business functions and activities. The following are some strategies that you could adopt for your business.

Cost leadership strategy

A cost leadership strategy is where the firm sets out to compete with rivals on the basis of low cost through obtaining several cost advantages. In this strategy, you will be aiming to become the lowest cost producer in the industry or market.

A firm would charge prices equal to or below the market price in an attempt to capture a larger customer base and drive higher growth. However, that may not always be the case. The key emphasis of a cost leadership is to produce goods at the lowest cost possible.

The aim of the firm is to build and organize a seamless flow of operations that enable costs to stay minimal. Some of the ways through which this can be done is by opting for cheaper sourcing of raw materials, attaining staff and process efficiencies, efficient outsourcing, vertical integration and economies of scale and scope.

However, a cost leadership strategy is not without limitations. Those who may intend to use a low-cost strategy should bear in mind that rivals, over time, may be able to cut costs as well and be able to dictate lower prices.

This is because as companies mature, they are able to achieve economies of scale that pushes costs down. Furthermore, the availability of newer technology and suppliers charging lower input costs could also limit the effectiveness of your low costs.

Hence, a cost-leadership strategy could prove useful in the short-term but will only be effective in the long-term if newer ways of obtaining cost advantages are pursued and implemented. Otherwise, your business can lose significant market share over time.

DIFFERENTIATION STRATEGY

In a differentiation strategy, emphasis is put on making your brand of goods and services distinct from those of competitors. Due to this unique packaging of your business identity and brand, you can increase your bargaining power and set higher prices in the market.

How you choose to differentiate will depend entirely up to you and can also hinge on what resources or capabilities you have. For instance, in the case of a product, you can choose to offer quicker delivery of the product to the customer or offer other benefits such as flexible hours or higher product quality.

You should only pursue a differentiation strategy if you have access to proper scientific research and development fund, a highly experienced and skilled workforce and a reputation for innovation and quality.

A differentiation strategy will allow your business to stand out from the rest of competition. By making your products and services appear unique to the buyer, the high or premium price charged can help you offset the cost of production by a higher margin. Also, in a situation where suppliers increase the price of input prices, you can pass on the additional costs to the customer without suffering much risk of customers switching to a rival product.

Furthermore, a product or service that is differentiated by branding or altering its characteristics will be able to mitigate the threat of substitute products.

However, there are certain risks that must be borne in mind. First of all, the customers' preferences and needs may change over time due to cultural or technological influences that can undermine your brand's strength. Firms which follow a differentiation strategy should always keep track of constantly changing customer needs, wants and preferences to anticipate future trends.

Secondly, rivals can easily imitate your value proposition that can escalate competition. The example of Samsung's imitation of the design of Apple's devices led Samsung to considerable success. Although a long legal battle ensued, Samsung emerged as a great rival which eroded much of Apple's market share.

FOCUS STRATEGY

In a focus strategy, you have the option to pursue either a cost leadership strategy or a differentiation strategy except that a narrow segment or groups of segments will be targeted instead of all customers.

By choosing a smaller group of the market, you can almost hide your business from being preyed upon from more established players. You also have the benefit of enjoying higher customer profitability and loyalty. Although suppliers can gauge greater control over input prices, you are able to pass on the additional costs without fearing the threat of close substitutes.

Furthermore, as volumes will be lower owing to the smaller size of the target audience, your business can be far more flexible and agile to customer needs and wants and be able to serve them better than rivals who target everyone.

However, there are risks that rivals can carve out sub-segments of your target audience and erode your market share and profitability. Also, firms who have higher volumes can make use of various cost and other competitive advantages due to economies of scale which smaller businesses cannot. This can allow them to adapt their products to the segment you have chosen to target and capture market share.

WHICH STRATEGY TO FOLLOW?

Whatever strategy you choose will have far reaching consequences for your business. Therefore, it is very important that the right business strategy is chosen. It must also be stated that only one strategy should be followed. Following more than two strategies will not be wise to effectively utilize resources and capabilities.

For example, a firm cannot simultaneously follow both a cost leadership strategy and a differentiation strategy as the activities and goals required to achieve the outcomes will be conflicting. Cost leadership requires considerable operational efficiency requirements while differentiation, on the other hand, requires a great degree of creativity and innovation.

To choose the strategy that is relevant for your business, you will need to evaluate it using the previously mentioned tools of SWOT analysis and 5 forces framework. In terms of the SWOT analysis, the correct strategy will be the one that gives you the greatest leverage by maximizing the strengths and opportunities and minimizing the weaknesses and threats.

Whereas, the objective of the 5 forces model will be to highlight how you can position your business in a way that reduces competitive pressures and optimizes bargaining power.

SMART GOALS

Once the right strategy is determined and chosen for your business, the next thing to do is to set SMART goals that reflect the decided strategy. Despite many of the departmental goals that can differ in relation to its type and function, goals which are important for the overall health of the business pertaining to survival and growth must be decided upon.

SMART goals can help you do this. A SMART goal is any which is the following:

1. **S**pecific
2. **M**easurable
3. **A**chievable
4. **R**ealistic
5. **T**imely

SPECIFIC

A specific goal is easier to achieve than a general one. Specificity can be increased by determining:

- What needs to be accomplished?
- Where it needs to be accomplished?
- When it needs to be accomplished?
- What are the requirements and conditions for the goal?
- What are the reasons or benefits for achieving the goal?

MEASURABLE

A measurable goal is any that can be easily monitored and evaluated. It is important that any goal that you set out to achieve can be analysed and assessed without any difficulty to reward your employees on how efficiently they have worked. A measurable goal is one that involves asking:

- How many employees will be working on the project?
- How much should be devoted to completing the project?

ACHIEVABLE

Goals can be made achievable by looking at the resources and capabilities your business may have in terms of skill-set, new technology, excess capacity and land. When resources and capabilities are kept in mind, goals become far easier to achieve.

REALISTIC

A goal must also be realistic. That is, a goal must be relevant according the nature of your business and the capabilities you have and under the right time frames. It would not be realistic, for instance, to set goals that are outside the productive capacity of your employees. Also, a long-term goal that has no bearing or impact in the short-term can also be deemed as an unrealistic goal.

TIMELY

A goal should also conform to a particular time frame. If there is no time frame attached to a goal, then focus on completing the goal is lost. Therefore, depending upon how short or long term the goal is, an appropriate deadline should always be attached.

EXAMPLES OF GOALS

The goals which will be of relevance and importance to your business will depend on the information you have gathered from your market research and the amount of resources and capabilities that you possess. It is essential that sufficient time be given to ensuring that smart goals are in accordance with your willingness, capacity and ability to achieve the tasks.

Here are a few goals that can be of interest to your business.

BREAK-EVEN

If you have decided on starting a new venture or business, one of the most important of goals for you is to first break-even on the funds used to invest in the business. The quicker you can recoup the cost of your investment, the quicker you will earn profits and be able to grow at a rapid pace.

The break-even time will depend on what industry or market you have entered. If the market requires considerably high amount of investments pertaining to equipment, technology and facilities, then the longer it will take for you to break even and vice versa.

PROFITABILITY

Whilst break-even is important, you must never lose sight of your profitability. Especially if a cost-leadership strategy is chosen, maintaining a strong grip on costs will be critical in helping you achieve your goals. It may be that your business is making good sales but costs are simply too high for sufficient profits to be made.

Moreover, the higher the profitability, the quicker you will be able to break-even. You can choose a host of cost-reduction targets such as reducing overheads by 10% in the next 6 months or choosing a net profit margin increase between 5% and 10%.

CUSTOMER AND EMPLOYEE RETENTION

The goal of improving customer retention rates will be a lifeline for your business. Without any customers, your business will have neither future growth nor survival. On the converse, greater customer retention rates will mean greater customer loyalty and brand consolidation.

You can focus on improving customer retention rates in a number of ways. If you have a website, you can keep an eye out for higher conversion rates that will indicate the number of your website visitors who actually became your customers.

In other cases, you can instruct your sales department a set of sales targets every month or so. They can employ sales calls to different clients or initiating face-to-face meetings as a way of acquiring new customers and influencing higher retention rates.

MARKET SHARE GROWTH

It may also be important for your business to focus on increasing its market share. Through the use of the 5 forces framework, which you can use to position your business effectively, you can secure a competitive edge over the competition from the onset and build your market share.

Quarterly market share evaluations will prove essential in staying informed of the threat of competition and how well your business is coping with the challenges faced in the market.

IMPORTANCE OF MONITORING AND EVALUATING YOUR GOALS

Your SMART goals will only be effective if you take the necessary time and resources to constantly evaluate and monitor how well the business activities are conforming to it. It is, furthermore, essential that goals be routinely and periodically evaluated to identify areas of concern and take quick corrective action.

Therefore, you can have supervisors or department managers supervise their subordinates and ensure that all tasks are carried out efficiently and due accountability is exercised. Furthermore, weekly and monthly meetings should also be arranged to discuss the challenges faced in various departments and as a business on the whole.

Regular meetings will keep motivation and accountability in flow and goals that have been set can be achieved with greater confidence.

PRIORITIZING FINANCIAL AND NON-FINANCIAL PERFORMANCE INDICATORS

After you have decided on what goals and objectives are essential in helping you achieve your strategy, you are then required to pick certain performance indicators that can help you monitor the outcomes and results of business activities and decisions. Usually, this involves a set of financial indicators such as sales growth, gross profit margin and net profit margin.

This also consists of many investment appraisal techniques such as Return on Capital Employed (ROCE), Net Present Value (NPV) and Economic Value Added (EVA) used to assess the viability of a crucial investment decision.

However, equally if not more importantly, non-financial indicators are also vital in making accurate representations of business activities and its realities which can supplement better decision making and accountability in general. These include: brand value, word-of-mouth marketing, customer satisfaction, employee satisfaction and more.

In many instances, the financial performance of a certain activity may be poor, but the non-financial performance can be outstanding. Especially if long-term investment decisions have to be made, the initial outflow of cash in the form of capital investment and lack of any significant cash inflows can be interpreted as a substantially poor financial performance.

However, the long-term benefits it accrues to the business in terms of efficient business processes, higher employee productivity and customer loyalty are indications of a success. Therefore, it is essential that any business goal or activity undertaken is looked from a combination of financial and non-financial factors to accurately reflect the reality of the outcome.

If your business has decided on choosing a cost leadership strategy and is looking to invest in better machinery and equipment, then you can consider the immediate financial impact of the machine as well as the future implications on cost and productivity. Alternatively, if you have pursued a differentiation strategy, then any investment or business decision needs to be evaluated on the terms of improving and influencing higher innovation and creativity and uniqueness.

Furthermore, you must bear in mind that many of the aspects of non-financial factors are intangible while those of the financial aspects are tangible. Making a decision based upon intangible factors can be difficult and misleading. You can thus attempt to bridge the gap by regularly conducting surveys and market research.

So for instance if the results of a new product launch activity show high customer satisfaction and loyalty via surveys and other focus group studies, a business can conclude that the activity was a success based upon the tangible reality of a non-financial factor.

CHAPTER 3: PLANNING

A business plan is a written record of a firm's business goals, the nature of the business and the departmental strategies employed to achieve the overall objectives. These departmental strategies involve sales, marketing, operations, finance, management accounting and other areas of the business.

The aim of the business plan is to serve as a road map providing useful guidance on how each business function should be performed effectively and efficiently. This enables managers to become familiar with the tasks at hand and to anticipate how various activities should be prepared for.

OPERATIONS

The operations function is primarily concerned with the efficient coordination and utilization of resources in conducting activities from production to delivery. Operation managers are tasked with ensuring that all business activities flow smoothly and that customers' needs and wants are met in terms of high quality, reliability and speed.

Your strategy will influence how your operations ought to be organized.

No-frills or deluxe operations

Operations can compliment business goals in different ways. There needs to be a right match between the overall strategy and the flow of activities in the operations process of a business. So depending upon what strategy the firm chooses, the operations process should be a direct reflection of it.

Take the famous low cost, British airliner, Ryanair. It is well-known for its cost leadership strategy which means that keeping costs low are given the utmost importance which results in lower prices for passengers. Its seamless and fast operations process eliminates unnecessary waste such as time.

There are no long waiting queues for flights, tickets are booked and bought online and flight routes are kept short for quick, low cost flight service. There are no meals provided on the plane nor are there any in-flight entertainment options. However, this particularly no-frills feature is precisely what made Ryanair a big success.

Compare this with British Airways that is known for providing deluxe flight services to multiple destinations, in-flight entertainment options and more. It adopts a differentiation strategy and not cost leadership as highly branded deluxe services are provided in an effort to differentiate itself from other airliners.

How you choose to adopt your strategy will have a bearing on how your operations should be organized. If Ryanair, for instance, implemented the operations of British Airways whilst still keeping cost leadership its main objective, it will not be able to achieve its goals. Therefore, the right match should always be chosen.

PURCHASING

Purchasing or procurement is also an element of the operations function that includes purchase of raw materials, equipment and other items necessary for the production and distribution of the product or service.

If you are following a low-cost strategy, then raw materials or items that enable high quality of products and services will not be relevant to your business. However, technology, which may be somewhat expensive at first but can lead to significant cost reduction and smoother flow of business processes, will be important.

WAREHOUSING

Inventory storage is a critical area of operations. If warehousing capacity reaches its full, then a business is more exposed to risks in being unable to meet an increase in demand and experience greater overheads required for maintenance and lighting and heating.

If you are a start-up, then you can decide to invest in an enterprise resource planning tool (ERP). This will allow all of your inventory records, sales transactions and supply chain management system to be linked and accessed under one roof. An ERP tool can exhibit condensed reports on a daily basis that will allow better operational decision making and monitoring.

WASTE ELIMINATION

If you have an ERP system, you can use it to determine what the barriers to a seamless flow of activities are. However, if you do not have such as system at the moment, then it is advised to conduct regular meetings with heads of departments and discuss what kinds of barriers their respective departments are facing.

Elimination of waste involves making sure that activities are not disrupted by unnecessary time or that poor quality is not the outcome of its process.

RISK MANAGEMENT

It is also highly important that risk management strategies are taken into account when organizing operations. It is inevitable that business will face, in one way or another, many kinds of disturbances that can have a devastating impact on their operations and their business.

Incidents such as natural disasters or emergency situations such as terrorist attacks, electrical outages and building fires are some cases where contingency plans come in handy. Therefore, in the event of such cases, certain procedures should be instructed to staff and those involved to mitigate the effects of the damage and to resume business operations as soon as possible.

In the case of a building fire, exit signs should be placed and a safe passage to leave the premises should be communicated to all members of staff in advance. Also, fire extinguishers should also be placed close by to put out fires inside the premises.

MARKETING

Your marketing will be the cornerstone in increasing sales and profit growth opportunities by leveraging your resources and capabilities to effective use. It will be the key function for allowing your business to stand out in the market and fortifying your business from the threats of competition, substitute products and new entrants.

This is because the better the marketing, the more loyal your customers become to your brand and not your rivals'. How well you adopt marketing will determine whether you are a market leader or a market follower.

TARGET MARKET

Your marketing will not be effective unless you first choose what target market you wish to target to. This is because effectively satisfying customer's requirements can only be done if the marketing messages, strategies and tactics are in conformity with the needs of a specific buyer's persona. Without it, customer-focus will be lost and rivals can quickly outpace your business.

From the 5 forces model and other market research, a suitable market segment can be chosen that has sufficient income and is sizeable enough for sufficient gains to be realized. The customers' habits, preferences, likes and tastes must also be given special attention and should be incorporated into the marketing plans for decision making.

PRODUCT AND SERVICE CHARACTERISTICS

As it is very commonly assumed, marketing is not merely about promotion. Rather, it is a philosophy that informs decisions related to supply chain management and production requirements. Depending upon what strategy you choose, the product and service characteristics will vary.

For instance, if a differentiation strategy is adopted, then considerable amount of time and resources need to be given on making the product stand out from the competition in terms of quality and packaging. Quality considerations do not necessarily have to be about design; it can be the ease of handling, how environmentally friendly it is and more. This is unlike in the case of a cost leadership strategy where any emphasis beyond keeping costs low will not be emphasized as it will conflict with the overall objective of the business.

Packaging on the other hand will also be unique in a differentiation strategy. Attractive colours, brand logo and an appealing design could form the basis of quality packaging.

BRANDING AND ADVERTISING

Branding is a crucial aspect in marketing. Businesses that invest effort and time into making their brands well known and recognized usually enjoy greater customer loyalty and profits. It also helps to mitigate the competitive pressures from rival products and services and allow the firm to have a greater control over suppliers and customers through which it has a freer hand when it comes to price setting.

Branding, however, is relevant for those firms pursuing a differentiation strategy and not so much for a cost-leadership one. The objective of branding is to make the firm appear different from its competitors. It involves heavy advertising and marketing expenditure that would not be suitable for keeping costs low.

In addition to superior product and service characteristics, a unique customer experience should be displayed and marketed such as specifying user imagery that is, the type of customers the product will cater to along with logo design, tagline and consistent marketing theme. This will create a distinct brand personality.

If you have opted for a cost-leadership strategy, then all that you are competing on is price. Taking Ryanair's example as a low-cost airliner, it will not compete on the variety of destinations, the in-flight meals, entertainment options nor other services. It will only compete on low cost and prices offered to passengers.

Similarly, substantial amounts of capital will not be invested in creating a unique brand personality through heavy advertising. The utmost emphasis will be on making operational improvements in business processes and activities.

CUSTOMER-FOCUS

Marketing is essentially about satisfying customer requirements or needs in a profitable manner. Ignoring customers' needs and requirements will lead a business into decline. Therefore, whichever industry or market a business is operating in, it is important for it to know exactly what customers want in order to thrive.

In terms of customer-focus, the low cost business will limit customer focus to providing low prices for no-frills products or services. Attempting to fulfil any other variant of customer expectations can distort the strategy and impede its effectiveness. Low cost product or service that fulfils the basic need of a customer is high product quality or service for a cost-leadership strategy.

A differentiated business, on the other hand, will keep a close eye on the changing customer needs and preferences and will opt to fulfil their needs. This is especially important as the features on which the company or brand distinguishes itself may change overtime that can lead to significant losses for the company.

It may employ regular market research in the form of surveys, focus groups, industry reports and other research to be fully aware of the changing market dynamics.

DIGITAL MARKETING

In the age of computers and gadgets, one cannot ignore the importance of digital marketing. It not only is cheaper in comparison with non-traditional methods and means of marketing, but also it can allow products and services to be marketed to people across multiple cities and countries.

A low cost business will employ a heavier use of digital marketing tools and methods to increase its business visibility and make greater profits and sales. Tools such as SEO, PPC, lead generation, website marketing, marketing automation and data analytics are just some of the most commonly used means to export its business value to customers.

New expensive technologies may also be considered for purchase provided that it can lead to higher cost savings and business process simplification. Tools such as ERP, Cloud computing services and data mining are all technologies that are applicable to both low cost and differentiated businesses.

SALES

A company's sales strategy is vital for finding new customers, acquiring and retaining them for the long-term and ensuring that multiple streams of revenue are secured. Usually, a company's sales strategy is made over the long term that consists of multiple years that is then broken down into annual and monthly targets. This is done so that the sales team can target the right people consistently to grow the business whilst also retain existing customers.

A business, regardless of which strategy it chooses, first needs to know the details about the customer. What do customers demand? What are their basic needs? And what are their expectations? These are just some of the questions that may be important to sales managers. Based on this information, the right customers need to be then targeted that can be an important source of revenue for the business.

 The sales function will be more relevant, however, to the business that employs product or service characteristics other than cost; in other words, a differentiated business. Commercial products such as technical equipment and technologies for instance may require sales teams to communicate the value of their product to other business customers. The same is applicable for consumer products and services such as clothing, banking, catering services and more.

Customers need to be directed to how the product or service can fulfil their needs and task and how its features are superior to those offered by rivals and substitutes. It is important that all sales promotions are done from the mind of a customer.

Sales representatives that only describe the features of the product or service alone will not be able to win the minds of customers. Instead, they need to know the issues facing the customer and how the product or service can benefit them.

SALES METHODS

There are number of ways the sales function can materialise. Depending upon how your organisation or start-up business is organised, there are two methods which you need to be aware of: direct and indirect sales. Direct sales refers to face-to-face contact with a customer while indirect sales refers to selling products or services through third party websites, market channels and distributors.

Indirect sales methods are generally cheaper to use due to low maintenance and set up costs. Selling your products or services on platforms which are well-known to customers is also an added advantage in increasing business visibility and establishing credibility.

However, indirect sales methods are not ideal for developing business-client relationships. With a substantial amount of website visitors, purchase decisions can also become difficult for customers.

In contrast, direct sales methods are ideal for developing and maintaining customer relationships. Face-to-face two-way interactions between sales representatives and customers can help your business to understand the issues, challenges, requirements and preferences of your customer. This can help your sales team become more customer-focused and understand how exactly customers' needs ought to be fulfilled.

Moreover, direct sales techniques are also good for tackling the competition head-on. Customers can be given information on how rivals' products do not conform to the needs of the customer and how your product or service is superior.

Questions asked from the customer can be answered in a quick and convincing manner, unlike in indirect sales methods.

There are also cost-effective digital software applications for increasing your business' sales pipeline. Methods such as lead generation techniques, for instance, direct already interested customers to your website. The higher the leads, the more chance your business has of acquiring new customers.

Marketing automation systems can track leads on a multi-channel platform via website, social media and email. This can allow you to know which channel is most effective in capturing leads so that you can devote most of your time on areas that can result in optimal sales and profits.

HR AND TRAINING

The human resources function should not be taken lightly. After all, a business is driven and measured by the capabilities, skills and experience of its staff. If capable and resourceful staff is not hired, whatever strategy you set for your business, you will not see it come to fruition.

This is because your employees are the ones directly or indirectly interacting and conversing with your end customers. It is your employees who manage limited resources, develop contingency plans for better risk management and ensure that all operations, marketing and finances are in control.

HIRING THE RIGHT PEOPLE

The HR manager needs to be familiar with the organisation's business strategy. Careful evaluation must be done to ensure that the right people are hired to achieve the company's strategic goals and objectives. If your business is opting for business that offer superior customer service, then employees with great interpersonal and communication skills need to be hired.

However, if your business claims to sell high quality products, then employees with technical skills and production methods such as engineers, designers, architects, for instance, need to be employed.

Efficient employees are also important for a low cost business. This is because higher worker productivity will only help to bring down costs and expenses that otherwise would not be possible.

EMPLOYEE MOTIVATION

Keeping your employees motivated is also an important role of HR. Without motivation, your employees will not be willing to put the extra effort and help achieve your business targets. This can cause your business to lose its competitive edge and allow rivals to take the lead.

It always helps to organise outdoor activities such as a field trip, set one-to-one counselling sessions and promote opportunities for employees to grow professionally. It is also essential the barriers to demotivation are identified and countered.

EMPLOYEE TRAINING

Employee training is a crucial aspect of the HR role in order that the right skill-sets, leadership and other qualities and competencies are cultivated within staff according to the changing market dynamics and requirements.

For example, it may be that marketing and operations is increasingly becoming infused with technology adoption. If this is the case in your market or industry, it will be necessary for you to train your staff to use the latest equipment and tools.

There are a series of steps to ensure that your training policy meets results.

Firstly, structure and deliver workshops and seminars aimed at highlighting specific skills that employees are lacking or failing at in their performance appraisals. Through these programs, employees will not only become motivated to do better at work, but also help them acquire valuable skills that will help them advance higher in their career ladder.

Secondly, identify professional training bodies and institutes that offer valuable skills that are crucial for employee productivity and growth. Institutes such as the Dale Carnegie Training deliver a wide range of courses aimed to build skills such as interpersonal skills, sales training and leadership.

A specific set of courses could then be offered that are considered highly relevant to your organisation or business activity. This could be made more convenient and access by using administrative software such as the Learning Management System. In this, each employee can create his or her own account that will provide all the details regarding the courses on offer, data of courses and fees if applicable.

Moreover, sufficient monitoring and performance evaluation mechanism needs to be followed so that employees can be measured on how well they have demonstrated their newly acquired skill in a business setting.

Alternatively, HR could also employ job rotation and job enrichment initiatives. Job rotation, ideally used for trainees, refers to assigning interns or trainees to projects of different departments and functions. This allows considerable skills as well as familiarity with different business processes and activities.

Upon a success job rotation program, employees emerge as leaders knowing full well how different activities and functions should be performed. This leads to better coordination and communication between staff and helps break down work barriers.

Job enrichment, on the other hand, involves making the jobs less repetitive and more challenging for the employee. This allows employees to learn new skills and qualities and is ideal for eliminating worker boredom. The greater challenges and responsibilities placed on the employee' shoulders, the greater the degree of confidence that leads to higher job satisfaction and job efficiency.

MANAGEMENT ACCOUNTING

Management accounting refers to the collection and recording of key financial and accounting information that forms the basis for managerial decision making. In essence, management accounting is using current and future financial information to solve current business problems and counter anticipated risks.

Management accounting, thus, is a key area for analysing and assessing that all business activities and functions conform to your business' overall goals and objectives.

CASH FLOW MANAGEMENT

The cash flow of a business highlights the overall health of the business. It is considered the bloodline of a business and any problems associated with it can signal great dangers for your business.

The cash flow forecast shows the business' cash flowing into the business (cash inflows) with respect to the cash flowing out of it (cash outflows). For best practices, a business would want its cash inflows to offset its cash outflows.

A cash flow forecast is not the same as a profit and loss account. This means that whatever your cash flow situation is, it does not indicate whether your business will be profitable or not. For instance, a business could have a healthy cash flow situation but still incur a loss throughout the year as a whole.

Businesses should take utmost care in ensuring that their cash flow position is adequate. Buying relevant machinery, equipment and other items can be necessary for a business but too much of it can increase your cash outflow and reduce your cash inflow.

In such as case, your business can adopt a set of approaches and techniques to limit cash outflows as much as possible through:

1. Taking payment in full immediately from customers
2. Delaying payment to suppliers and other third parties
3. Learning to detect cash flow crises before it happens

A monthly cash flow budget or cash budget can also be set a target of the minimum amount of cash to be spent for each month. Setting such targets can help enforce discipline and accountability – two necessary ingredients for a good cash flow position.

BUDGETING

Budgets are an effective way of ensuring that your strategic goals and objectives are met effectively and efficiently. A variety of different budgets can be set that can act as a roadmap pertaining to how you should utilise resources for maximum benefit and leverage. For each budget, a set of performance targets can be set that once achieved can ensure that your business strategy is being implemented properly.

Here are some examples of common budgets found in many businesses.

- Production budget
- Marketing budget
- Sales budget
- Expenses budget and more

CAPITAL BUDGETING

Capital budgeting or investment appraisal are a set of methods used to determine how worthwhile it is to make long term investments such as purchasing new machinery, land, plants, products, research development projects and so on. Long-term investments are an integral part of every business and deciding which investment gives off higher value can have significant consequences for the business.

To keep things brief, the following three methods will be briefly explored: payback method, accounting rate of return and net present value.

1) *Payback method*

This method is the simplest of investment appraisal techniques and is popular with small businesses for helping them decide which investment will be worthwhile. It refers to the time taken for the cash outflow of an investment to be recouped by the total number of cash inflows generated by the investment.

It is represented by the following formula:

Payback period = Initial investment / Cash inflows per period

An example of this can be a company that is deciding on investing in a land worth £150,000 and anticipates that the investment will generate £20,000 every year. Using the aforementioned formula will give a payback period of 5 years. This means that the cost of the investment can be recovered within 5 years.

With this formula, a company can compare and choose from multiple investment projects and the one with the shortest payback period will be the one that will be most worthwhile. However, businesses that are keen on using this method should also be aware of many of the inconsistencies in the method as it does not factor cash inflows after the payback period nor does it give consideration to the time value of money.

For instance, a business could deem an investment opportunity appropriate based on the projected cash inflows but not consider that it may reduce significantly later on. Also, the value of money does not stay consistent for many years as factors such as inflation cause the value of money to fall overtime.

2) *Accounting rate of return*

This method is considered a better alternative to the payback period as it takes into account the overall yield of the investment, something that payback period does not consider. To work out the accounting rate of return, one must add all the cash inflows of the investment, then deduct the amount of the investment from the figure and divide it by the number of years and then express it as a percentage.

It is represented by the following formula:

(Total projected cash inflows – cost of investment) x
100
Number of years

Although this method takes a little longer to calculate, its consideration of the total project cash inflows makes it more accurate than the payback period. For a small or large business that has plenty of investment opportunities, the ARR with the highest percentage will be the one to be pursued.

This means that the one with the shortest time for recovering the cost of investment will not necessarily be chosen and an investment project that takes many more years than another project can be worthwhile to invest.

3) *Net present value*

The net present value perhaps the most accurate of all investment appraisal techniques. While calculating the value of an investment is often more complicated than the aforementioned methods, its consideration of the time value of money as well as the total yield of the investment makes it an accurate evaluation tool for making investment decision making.

The formula is represented as the following:

Present value
= $\dfrac{A}{(1+r)^n}$

'A' refers to the project cash inflows generated per year, 'r' refers to the discount rate used to calculate the value of money and 'n' refers to the number of years. After the present value is found, the net present value is calculated by deducting the present value from the initial cost of capital investment. If the result is positive, then the investment is favourable for investment.

QUALITATIVE FACTORS

To make a well-rounded and accurate investment decision, you should also take into account non-financial factors that can have both long term and short term implications on your investment decision. Any business operates in a specific market environment and staying informed and considerate of various external factors can have a direct impact upon your profitability and sales potential.

Factors such as state of the economy, inflation and an expected increase in raw material costs, for instance, are some external factors that every business must be aware of. Other qualitative factors, such as legislation, market competitiveness, impact on branding and word-of-mouth marketing and level of technological prowess are other factors that can deem an investment favourable or unfavourable.

Furthermore, external costs such as costs of damage to the environment (e.g. pollution), public relations and loss of customer confidence are also other key factors that can influence decision making.

It may be the case that an investment decision is characterised by conflicting quantitative and qualitative factors. For example, an investment opportunity may be worthwhile in terms of financial numbers but unfavourable from a qualitative point of view. In such a case, a business must decide on its goals and objectives and refer back to its overall corporate strategy as a way to reconcile its decision making.

CHAPTER 4: EXECUTION

The execution involves ensuring that all planned objectives and activities are effectively and efficiently executed without incurring any pitfalls or delay. Many entrepreneurs come up with great ideas, make great well-thought out plans and strategies and even have access to the right tools and resources. However, they fail miserably in execution.

Execution is the second half of a strategy and is concerned with putting your human resources to effective use. This involves following a carefully planned framework in which the planned activities or goals of a company effectively match the individual goals of employees. Effective execution of strategic goals and objectives will hinge on the right leadership and a set of tactics to ensure that your strategy is implemented properly.

COMMON EXECUTION PITFALLS

There are many reasons why well planned out strategies fail to materialise. No matter how incredible your product or service characteristics are, there are still chances you can fail at executing your strategy. Here are some common pitfalls.

Poor or lack of proper communication

Proper communication is essential in ensuring that all necessary information and data that are useful in fulfilling the tasks are made known to employees. Businesses that do not have effective communication channels or mechanisms in place to allow employees to coordinate and cooperate with one another will fail at achieving the necessary goals and objectives.

More importantly, the employees' job description, roles, responsibilities and duties need to be clear to avoid any confusion. Many a time a business strategy fails to achieve fruition because the employees responsible for achieving it were not sure how they ought to contribute in their respective departments.

An overwhelming or meaningless plan

Another factor that causes strategy execution to fail is when the plan is overwhelming to follow. Entrepreneurs or CEOs of companies need to be careful not to make business plans and strategies too complex to follow. While it is important not to leave out important details that can affect the business competitively and financially, it is also worth pointing out that plans be realistic based upon the capabilities and skills of your employees.

This is why the importance of SMART goals should not be undermined as any plan that is realistic, achievable and timely will make practical sense for your staff to execute.

Alternatively, a plan should also not be meaningless to your employees. Plans that carry little practical value will not resonate deeply within employees as they will not have any idea how to achieve it in realistic terms.

Lack of proper monitoring and accountability

Perhaps the most important out of all execution pitfalls is the lack of monitoring, evaluation and accountability in ensuring plans or strategies are executed effectively. No matter how carefully thought out your strategy or plan is, if there are no measures in place to make sure it is going on track and is being implemented properly, the strategy holds little value to a business.

Furthermore, accountability, in terms of reward and punishment mechanisms, is also important for execution. Performance management, supervision, weekly meetings all plays an important role in keeping employees accountable and on edge in delivering output and for executing strategy successfully.

In light of the aforementioned pitfalls, there are many ways businesses can ensure that their strategy or plans are executed successfully. The following are four ways you can use to ensure your business strategy is executed without any mishaps.

1. Effective employee management
2. Quality leadership
3. Monitoring and evaluation
4. Alignment between strategy and culture

1) EMPLOYEE MANAGEMENT

There is no doubt that your employees will be the most important agents in executing your strategy. Along with the right management, they need the right leadership and communication platforms to steer them to the right direction in their activities. Here are a few ways employees can be utilised most efficiently for strategy execution.

INVOLVE THEM IN THE PLANNING PROCESS

As an entrepreneur, it can often be natural to make all the decisions yourself. However, when starting up a business, it can be very beneficial to seek ways to inspire and motivate your employees to become heavily involved in their work and invest in their efforts. One such way is to include them in the planning process itself.

Your employees are your most valued assets. Involving them in the planning process will communicate to them what the company intends to accomplish in the future and how the employees can play an active role in that accomplishment. Furthermore, it can also prevent times of crises as employees will not feel overwhelmed but rather anticipated it and prepared themselves to meet the goals.

IMPROVE TRANSPARENCY

The more transparent your business processes and activities are, the more productive and valued your employees will feel in their work and deliver greater output. Many entrepreneurs who set up their businesses usually overlook this part of the business and then wonder why their employees are not performing up to their standards.

One important first step is to provide an induction to the company, familiarise them of their roles and responsibilities and always be a helping hand to support their enquiries and challenges. You must also not forget to discuss and explain strategy and its details so no element of doubt or confusion is left on the minds of workers.

A lot of the times, strategies fail to execute because employees were not sure what their job responsibilities and duties were. Therefore, your workers will have more clarity and will have less chances of committing mistakes. The more transparent your business is, the more chances your employees have of being more productive and executing strategies efficiently.

STRENGTHEN EMPLOYEE ACCOUNTABILITY

Whilst it is important to foster employee motivation and productivity, it is also important that bad apples be distinguished from the right ones. This means that proper performance evaluation needs to be conducted to assess past employee performance results as well as their output in times of crisis.

Employees can be encouraged to internalise strategy in their day to work jobs. This will be particularly useful if you want to influence certain behaviours of employees. Therefore, for those who exhibit signs of strategic thinking there can be a range of reward options.

Furthermore, the right action needs to be taken against those who have performed poorly. An inefficient employee can bring the business down and dismissing them will send a clear message about employee accountability.

You can also make constant use of dashboards and other reminder tools which your eyes will fall upon and be reminded of your targets and responsibilities.

PROVIDE EMPLOYEE COACHING

Employee coaching is an important part of encouraging your employees to deliver their best and outdo their own limits. You first have to analyse and determine which important skills are lacking and what particular skill-set and qualities are required to best execute business strategy.

After determining what is lacking, you can organise a seminar or workshop by inviting a specialist speaker or instructor to train your employees.

2) EFFECTIVE LEADERSHIP

Much has been written and spoken about the importance of leadership for influencing organisational and team success. Some of the best companies known today have been able to pull their sinking ship from heavy storms due to the praiseworthy attributes of its leaders.

The late Apple co-founder and former CEO, Steve Jobs, was a prime example of having the vision, passion and dedication to make a turnaround for the company and allow it to become one of the greatest brands in business history. Other more recent business leaders known for their remarkable leadership and great business acumen include Jeff Bezos of Amazon, Richard Branson of Virgin Group and Larry Page from Google.

No one leader will have the same leadership style, some may be autocratic, some maybe transactional and others maybe transformational. All have their uses and it is the job of a leader to know which style will help him or her get the best results.

STYLES OF LEADERSHIP
Autocratic leadership

In this style, a leader assumes responsibility in carrying out his or her duties without consulting the employees. An autocratic leader will closely supervise workers and will ensure tasks are fulfilled as quickly as possible.

Although this style allows tasks to be carried out quickly, it suffers from causing employee dissatisfaction and inhibiting employee creativity and innovation. CEOs or managers who value employee contribution and motivation must think twice before adopting such an approach.

Transactional leadership

In a transactional leadership style, the leader and employee both work on mutually agreed goals and priorities whereby the leader has the authority to reward or punish his or her workers. This style is particularly useful for providing clarity to both parties and for ensuring that best practice is maintained.

However, this leadership style also lacks the support structure for cultivating creativity and innovation in employees.

Transformational leadership

This is where the leader will seek to increase the motivation and satisfaction level of his or her employees and be directly engaged with them to ensure organisational tasks and responsibilities are fulfilled properly. This style is especially useful for improving employee productivity and motivation.

NEW LEADERSHIP APPROACHES

In addition to the aforementioned styles, there are also new approaches to leadership that can prove valuable in executing strategies and meeting business goals and objectives. Here are a few.

Assess your workers

A leader needs to adopt a particular leadership style or attitude in accordance with the skill level of his or her workers. A failure to match the right fit between the leadership style and staff skill-set can be detrimental to your business. For example, if employees are highly motivated but unskilled or semi-skilled, the leader must focus on briefing them with the necessary information to reduce risks and constraints and provide coaching.

On the other hand, if the employees are highly skilled but have low motivation, then the leader should adopt a more transformational leadership style whereby employee satisfaction and motivation will be maintained.

Know what works for your business

You should also have a good idea of what works for your business. If the nature of your business is such that time is of the essence and quick decisions need to be taken, then a direct or autocratic leadership style will be most suitable in keeping things under control and ensuring that unnecessary time is not wasted. However, if ample time is required for creativity and innovation to manifest, then you will have to inspire them with your vision and goals.

Anticipate future trends

As mentioned previously, a good leader is one who adopts a leadership style in accordance with the skill level of employees and the nature of the business. It is important for you to recognise that you cannot maintain the same leadership style over the long-term. In the case of a young start-up company where employees are new to the company, a leader can choose to give them less autonomy.

However, overtime, when employees have attained enough experience and skills, the leader can decide to give them more control over their work and encourage a more participative culture. In such a culture, input from experienced workers can be taken with utmost seriousness and frankness and can even be given permission to train or manage new employees.

Therefore, a good leader is one that adapts his or her leadership style or mind-set in lieu of his or her environment.

LEADERSHIP COMMUNICATION METHODS

There is more to a leader than just the type of leadership style he or she adopts in steering the business to success. There are also a host of communication methods that facilitate in galvanising the employees to deliver results with great zeal and commitment. It is the job of leader to nurture the talents of each of his or her employees and to navigate it to executing strategy.

Here are the common methods of effective leadership communication.

1. *Personify your leadership*

It is worth noting that your employees are neither slaves nor robots and so are sensitive to emotions. When you personalise your messages and instructions to your employees, the more effectively it will be received. This is important as meaningful relationships are integral to successful business outcomes. While it is important to maintain professionalism and work-based culture in a business, it does not hurt in getting personal with your employees.

Doing so will help you establish your credibility as a leader and gain their trust and respect more easily. This will allow goals and objectives to be met with greater commitment as your employees will enjoy taking part in carrying out their duties and responsibilities.

2. *Specify your demands*

A second method to improve your communication with your subordinates is to clearly specify your instructions or requirements to your staff. It is critical that your messages and the tone you use for voicing your thoughts and emotions do not contain any elements of ambiguity and that your staff can clearly understand what you want out of them.

Giving concise and to the point instructions will be understood better by your employees and assist them in achieving their tasks.

3. *Use empathy where necessary*

Empathy is one word we are not accustomed to when we talk about CEOs of large multinational corporations or businesses in general. Rather, it is more common to find it in domains of psychology and therapy. However, increasingly we find that more and more lexicons and definitions of behavioural psychology are being infused with business management and leadership.

This is because empathy is an important characteristic of a leader who wishes to see his or her subordinates pass their hurdles and overcome their barriers. In many instances, employees can face great difficulties in fulfilling their roles and duties and a simple pat on their back is all that is needed for them to outshine themselves.

Qualities of compassion, care and love are attributed to empathy and such an approach can do wonders for stimulating motivation and dedication within employees. For a leader to show empathy does not necessarily entail that he or she approves of the conditions or circumstances of his or her employees.

Instead, the leader appreciates and understands the problems or difficulties they face and encourages them to take the right action.

4. *Know what you are talking about*

Leaders should also have good command of the field in which they are leading their teams of employees. The mark of a distinguished leader is that they lead with knowledge, experience and integrity. If you as an entrepreneur do not know the intricate details of your field, you will not be able to communicate the task properly to your subordinates.

5. *Cultivate logical and analytical thinking*

It is important that business leaders cultivate a culture of rational thinking and improving the analytical abilities of their employees. The overwhelming amount of accessibility to data and information means that businesses are becoming more data-driven in their functions and activities.

It is thus essential that leaders demonstrate analytical thinking and require employees to think on their feet. Leaders should always demand that employees come up with new ways to solve business problems by backing up with research and practical solutions.

3) MONITORING AND EVALUATION

The importance of monitoring and evaluating your activities cannot be overstated. If you do not know how well you are performing and how it is impacting on your financial and non-financial KPIs, then there is simply no point in running your business. Frequent assessment of your activities can help you trace problems and areas of concern early on that will prevent it from snowballing into larger and complex challenges.

A monitoring and evaluation mechanism can cover important details spanning multiple functions and departments. For example, it can reveal important insights pertaining to new and anticipated threats and opportunities which were not taken into account when formulating the business strategy. This will allow you to adapt your activities to changes and have a lead over competitors.

It also allows serving as a tool for measuring employee productivity and keeping them engaged in achieving business targets. If you have strategic goals and objectives that you wish to be completed, then monitoring and evaluation is highly critical for obtaining success.

DEVELOPING A MONITORING SYSTEM

Monitoring is concerned with finding out if things are going to plan by collecting all the data and other information necessary. Developing a monitoring system would mean formulating a mechanism through which data collection and useful information can be obtained easily and on a regular basis.

For example, if you are operating a fast food restaurant then you would require that monthly sales and profit data is tracked using EPOS and other IT tools. In other cases, a sales team may set weekly targets to measure its own performance and sustain its sales growth.

Hence, here are few tips on developing a monitoring mechanism.

1) *What data should be collected?*

The first thing you want to decide is what data is important for monitoring. Data for monitoring should be that which is relevant to your function or business, which can be easily processed and utilised and collected in a timely manner.

For data to be relevant, a business has to be both internally and externally consistent. Business leaders cannot simply just focus on their internal activities pertaining to their employees whilst disregarding the external factors such as competitor actions, market changes and new legislation.

Narrowing down what data is relevant to the business will help to eliminate unnecessary time wasted on information that provides little value to achieving business goals and objectives.

2) *How often should data be collected?*

You as an entrepreneur or CEO should also stipulate how often data should be collected for monitoring purposes. Your choice will vary according to the type of industry in which you operate your business.

For example, if your business operates in a market that is constantly undergoing changes such as the fashion industry, then weekly data collection will be critical to your line of business. Marketing will be heavily influenced by constant demand fluctuations, rival campaigns and activities and price of raw materials. Production and supply chain will equally be involving quick decision making on new designs, inventory management and raw material purchases.

In other cases, where external factors do not change as fast, a monthly or quarterly review will be sufficient.

3) *What data collection tools and processes will be effective for monitoring?*

First of all, your business must have sufficient transparency that will allow data to be collected from multiple functions. To make this easier, you can implement an ERP tool that can synthesise information pertaining to activities from multiple functions such as marketing, finance, supply chain and more.

Secondly, external information pertaining to market data and competitors' actions can be gathered using primary and secondary research data. For market trends and changes, monthly reports or industry related magazines will be immensely important.

EVALUATING YOUR DATA

Efficient monitoring should be followed by effective evaluation. Without proper evaluation, you will not be able to make sense of the data which you have collected and important insights will not translate into strategic decision making.

To conduct a proper evaluation, you can set weekly meetings to answer the following questions:

- How are targets being pursued?
- What challenges are we currently facing?
- What opportunities can we cater to? And more

The evaluation should help answer the challenges and threats faced by the business as well as the opportunities. The questions relating to new opportunities can be answered by referring back to the overall strategy of the business in terms of how well does it fit the business strategy.

4) ALIGNMENT BETWEEN YOUR STRATEGY AND CULTURE

Another reason why your strategy is not being executed properly is that your work culture is not in accordance with the strategy you have chosen. A misalignment can occur which cannot only prevent you from achieving your goals and objectives, but also can disrupt your operations.

Take the following example. Company A has a work culture where employees make and act on decisions quick and efficiently without making any interruptions. The work processes and operations flow smoothly and seamlessly and an autocratic leadership style is adopted as time is made the ultimate judge on performance. However, in lieu of the rising competition, the company decides to make innovation its new goal.

The company, therefore, requires its employees to come up with creative ideas to solve business problems as well as develop unique products and services in comparison with those of its rivals. The question is will this strategy work? No, it will not. This is because the culture required for executing it is not appropriate. Innovation links with an entirely different culture to the one the company has fostered.

To execute innovation, a democratic leadership style which values teamwork, discussion of ideas and opinions and risk taking will be more befitting. In the current culture of Company A, time is of the essence which will only conflict with the time-consuming activities of discussing ideas and thoughts of others and the time taken to develop unique products and services.

For entrepreneurs seeking to establish their business, this means that your chosen strategy should complement the workplace culture that you intend to cultivate. Once you have decided on your strategy, your HR practices need to be aligned with it so that all hiring and training activities develop a culture that best fits your strategy.

Therefore, it is highly essential that there be an alignment or right match between the strategy you have chosen and the workplace culture.

CONCLUSION

Starting a business is not as straightforward as it seems from the outside. It requires going through the right thought processes and steps to understand the environment around you so you may know the impact it will have on your business' profitability. Hence, using tools such as SWOT analysis and Porter's Five Forces model will prove invaluable in assessing the threats and opportunities for your business.

In addition, a business should be underpinned by a specific business strategy such as differentiation, cost-leadership or focus strategies. This will set the course of your business activities and any misalignment could prove costly for your business.

More importantly, entrepreneurs who are looking to establish their business must plan effectively and gather the details regarding each of their business' functions and how it should conform to the overall business strategy used.

If you would like to know more about how to achieve your business goals please visit http://www.strategizeyourbiz.com/

REFERENCES

1) Porter, M.E, 2008 *The Five Competitive Forces That Shape Strategy*, Harvard Business Review. January Issue, 1-18

2) R Tanwar, 2013. Porter's Generic Competitive Strategies. *IOSR Journal of Business and Management*, Volume 15, Issue 1, 11-17

3) Cousins, Lamming, Lawson, Squire 2008. *Strategic Supply Chain Management: Principles, Theories and Practice.* 1st Ed. Upper Saddle River, New Jersey: Prentice Hall Financial Times.

ABOUT US

Strategize Your Biz is a business consulting service focused on serving the comprehensive needs of start-up and micro businesses. Do you have a concept that needs translating into a plan? Are you an existing business that needs help in development? Strategize Your Biz will help you develop an effective business strategy what will give you a clear vision, set objectives, plan towards your goals and execute in accordance with specific timelines whatever stage of the business growth cycle your business is positioned.

For more information on how to get started contact us. Let us take away the pain of business planning. So you can concentrate on the good stuff.

www.ingramcontent.com/pod-product-compliance
Lightning Source LLC
Chambersburg PA
CBHW040840180526
45159CB00001B/256